THE FIRST TIME HOME BUYERS PLAYBOOK

Insider secrets, strategies, and tips you must know to tackle the home buying process successfully.

© **Copyright 2018 by**_____- **All rights reserved.**

This document is geared towards providing exact and reliable information in regards to the topic and issue covered. The publication is sold with the idea that the publisher is not required to render accounting, officially permitted, or otherwise, qualified services. If advice is necessary, legal or professional, a practiced individual in the profession should be ordered.

- From a Declaration of Principles which was accepted and approved equally by a Committee of the American Bar Association and a Committee of Publishers and Associations.

In no way is it legal to reproduce, duplicate, or transmit any part of this document in either electronic means or in printed format. Recording of this publication is strictly prohibited and any storage of this document is not allowed unless with written permission from the publisher. All rights reserved.

The information provided herein is stated to be truthful and consistent, in that any liability, in terms of inattention or otherwise, by any usage or abuse of any policies, processes, or directions contained within is the solitary and utter responsibility of the recipient reader. Under no circumstances will any legal responsibility or blame be held against the publisher for any reparation, damages, or monetary loss due to the information herein, either directly or indirectly.

Respective authors own all copyrights not held by the publisher.

The information herein is offered for informational purposes solely, and is universal as so. The presentation of the information is without contract or any type of guarantee assurance.

The trademarks that are used are without any consent, and the publication of the trademark is without permission or backing by the trademark owner. All trademarks and brands within this book are for clarifying purposes only and are the owned by the owners themselves, not affiliated with this document.

TABLE OF CONTENTS

Introduction 1

Examining the First-Time Home Buyer Phenomenon 3

    Are You A First-Time Home Buyer? What Qualifies You As One? 3

    What Are The Standard Reasons First-Time Home Buyers Seek To Buy Homes? Are You Really Ready To Buy A Home? 5

Considerations You Should Have Before You Buy A Home 9

Being Able To Afford Your New Home 15

    Pre-Approval Loan Programs And Why They Make Sense For The New Buyer 15

What You Need To Have In Place So As To Get Approved For A Mortgage 18

    Financial Requirements For A Mortgage Approval: 18

    How Do You Save For A Down Payment On Your Very First House? 19

The Mortgage Question: The Ins & Outs Of Mortgage Financing ... 24

    A Brief Explanation on Mortgage Rates 24

    Shopping For A Mortgage: Steps To Finding Your Perfect Home Loan 26

    Using A Buyer Specialist 30

    Why Working With A Buyer Specialist Is Important 31

What Should The Ideal Buyer Specialist Do For You? 32

What Can You Do To Assist Your Buyer Specialist Find The Most Ideal Home Property For You? 35

Using A Home Buying Checklist To Get Your Ideal Home 37

The Home Buying Process: A How To Guide 42

Things You Should Know About Homes And Home Buying That Most Buyers Fail To Know 42

The 5 Best Kept Secrets With Regard To Home Buying 44

Do You Opt For Freehold Or Leasehold When Purchasing? A Look at Both and What You Can Expect From Them 45

A Step By Step Account On The Buying Process 49

Inspecting the Home: What Can You Expect? 56

Closing The Deal 60

The Concept Of "Earnest Money" Deposit 60

What Is An Earnest Money Deposit? 60

How Much Money Is Enough For The Earnest Money Deposit? 60

Protecting Your Earnest Money Deposit 61

The Process Of Negotiating The Contract: What Do You Do? ..61

What Exactly Happens At A Closing? 64

Comprehending Your Closing Process 65

How Much Cash Is Really Needed To Close On A Home? 67

Everything You Need To Know About the Various Closing Costs as a New Home Buyer 71

The Secrets to Coming Out On Top in a Bidding War 75

Financing Clauses: A Look At The Various Financing Clauses As You Will Find Them In The Closing Paperwork........................... 79

Action as a New Home Owner 83

Conclusion.. 85

INTRODUCTION

I want to thank you and congratulate you for downloading the book, *"The First Time Home Buyers Playbook: The Ultimate Guide To Successfully Buying Your First Home"*.

This book has actionable information on how to buy your first home seamlessly.

A home often means so very many things to its owner. It is a place where he or she lives with his/her family, first and foremost. It is a place where some of the most powerful memories are created. It is a place where Junior was born into, and every scratch on the wall, and subsequent repainting job, marks an ever-growing legacy. A home is also a great investment to have: simply owning a home can be the difference between being able to access a life-changing loan from your local bank, and having to accept your station in life and, in so doing, give up on dreams that have meant a lot to you. And if you ever have to sell your home in the future, homes are great in that they rarely, if ever, depreciate in value.

It is plain to see, thus, why so many buyers are daunted by the prospect of buying their new home. Will I pick the right home? What if I make a mistake and pick a home that is not ideal for me and mine? What do I need to buy a home? Are there extra costs that I do not know of that may unbalance my budget? How can I qualify for a mortgage? What do I do after I have closed the deal and have a new, unfamiliar home in my hands? These are all questions that may be going through your head. However, by the end of this book, you will not only have found deep answers to them, but you will be able to comfortably purchase home properties from now on, as well as give great advice to those who may seek it from you. Let's begin.

Thanks again for purchasing the book. I truly hope you enjoy it!

EXAMINING THE FIRST-TIME HOME BUYER PHENOMENON

Are You A First-Time Home Buyer? What Qualifies You As One?

This book has been crafted for the first-time homebuyer, although the nuggets of wisdom within will be practical for just about every kind of buyer. Is this your first time buying a home? If you are, then this is the book for you. What qualifies one as a first-time home buyer, however?

What traits will place other people; people with perhaps much more experience than you have on the home-buying subject, in the same 1st time home buyer bracket as you? You may be surprised to learn that you actually qualify as a first-time home buyer, despite having been involved in buying a home in the past.

Let us look at what the U.S. Department of Housing and Urban Development (HUD) has to say on being a first-time home buyer, and who qualifies as one:

- A single parent who owned a home with the ex-spouse while in the institution of marriage is a 1st time home buyer. According to the HUD, you could have been married for 20 years, and co-owned a principal residence with your ex-spouse, but once the marriage dissolves and you decide to go out house shopping on your own as a single parent, you are a 1st time home buyer.

- A person who has not owned a principal residence for 3 years or more qualifies as a 1st time home buyer. If you have been involved in the purchase of a home, at a previous time, but have not lived in it for a time that totals 3 years, then you will be considered a first-time home buyer, at least by the HUD's metric, the next time you decide to go house shopping. A spouse will also be considered a first time home buyer if he or she meets the above as well. If you have owned your residence for over 3 years while your spouse hasn't, you two can be considered to be first time home buyers.

- A displaced homemaker who has only previously owned a house with a spouse is considered a 1st time home buyer. The homemaker may have a wealth of information to delve into, once house shopping time comes around, and he/she may have a lot more resources to dip into compared to most people, but the HUD considers him or her a 1st time home buyer. While such a person really isn't a novice, he is technically a first-time home buyer and should there be any legal hurdles in place, he will be considered by the court as a 1st time buyer.

- A person who has only previously owned a principle place of residence that's not fixed permanently to any foundation according to the applicable regulations falls in the category of a 1st time home buyer.

- A person who has only owned property that was/is not in compliance with the state's, model or local codes; and which may not be brought into compliance for a cost that is less than that of constructing a permanent structure; qualifies as a 1st time home buyer.

The above discussion on what makes you a first time home owner must have been eye opening. You will understand why we had to start by defining who a first time home owner is as we go on with the book.

If you fit in the first home buyer category, you must be really excited about getting started in the home buying process. But before we get to that, we will discuss some reasons that could be driving you to buy a home so that you understand whether you are actually ready to purchase your first home.

What Are The Standard Reasons First-Time Home Buyers Seek To Buy Homes? Are You Really Ready To Buy A Home?

There are multiple reasons why people buy houses. Some are good/great reasons; reasons that are bound to personal goals that help the individual move forward and fare better in life.

Let us look at the standard reasons that the typical American may have for buying a home first. (Note that these may also double up as reasons WHY you should buy a home.)

Standard Reasons People Buy Homes

- *Fulfilling the American Dream*

Many people believe that the American dream is not complete without ownership of property. Think white picket fences, lush green lawns and a mailbox that the postman stuffs packages into every once a week. Some people even take it a step further and purchase several homes, all in the name of fulfilling the American dream and so long as they can afford it comfortably, there is no harm in it. Regardless, whether the typical American is purchasing his or her first home or the fifth one, there is a deep sense of pride in getting to own it.

- *Tax advantages*

One of the greatest perks that come with home ownership is this- qualified home interest and property tax are tax deductible, so you stand to save considerable amounts from the tax man. Still, you should make a point of speaking with your tax advisor or attorney every so often and request the freshest information regarding the same.

- *Investment potential*

For most people, the home turns out to be their greatest investment. The beauty with land and property is that no matter how intense the inflation gets, in the long run, value appreciation will always outpace inflation. Selling off your home in the future will almost always guarantee you something in the way of profits. And if anything, owning a home allows you to use it as equity, should the need comes up.

- *Stability*

Nothing else sets your roots in the way a house does and at some point, everyone craves stability. Owning your own home gives you a fixed neighborhood. It gives you community and schools that you can associate with and call your own. One of the reasons why it is so vital to screen multiple homes before settling for one is that your home determines what your neighborhood is and what facilities you have at your disposal.

- *The concept of "forced savings"*

When you buy a home on loan, then you will have to direct a portion of your savings toward paying off the loan principal. And here is where it gets interesting: do not consider this monthly amount as cost; consider this monthly payoff as a savings plan. Does this even make sense? Of course it does- by paying off your loan principal, you are simply paying yourself by building equity, and getting ever closer to fully owning an asset. When the day comes and you are ready to retire, your investment will prove to be very useful

Are You Really Ready To Buy A Home? Reasons Not To Buy A Home

Here are some poor reasons that way too many people have when considering buying a home. If they are part of your reason-package, re-evaluate them and see if they really are valid and important in meeting your goals in life:

- *Reason #1: External pressure*

When you get to a certain age, or start a family or simply just get married, there may be pressure on you to buy a home. Friends and family may have expectations of you; that it is time to settle down and own a house, complete with a picket fence and maybe a dog. The one person you should listen to most is yourself. Are you really ready to bear household costs? Is a house less of an asset and more of a burden at this stage in life? You need to understand if you are in any shape to own a home. And, you know, sometimes, waiting a few years may put you in a position where you are able to own a far superior home than you otherwise would have, if you had caved in to pressure and shopped for one before being ready.

- *Reason #2: You are in a financial situation where you qualify for a mortgage*

The bank may see you as a worthy borrower who can be comfortably be lent money for a home, but qualifying for a mortgage does not automatically mean that you are ready to own a home. It is often a very smart idea to address any debt and spending issues first before you go out and take up a mortgage. By doing so, you will prove to yourself that you are ready to handle the budget modifications that come with buying a home on loan.

Take your time and save up a down payment. Get really in control of your finances, so that you are truly able to afford a home. In the long run, this will be very beneficial.

- *Reason #3: You just graduated or got a new job*

You may just have graduated with a degree, a Master's degree or a doctorate degree or perhaps have a new job lined up in place. However, this does not mean that the time is come to line up a new home as well. This is an amateur mistake too many people make, and then when something unexpected happens, such as getting transferred to a new state 3 years into their job, they are left in the ownership of a home, which does not suit their present circumstances. Take your time; rent at first and give it a couple of years before you consider buying a home. By then, you will have enough experience and knowledge to help you make an educated decision.

- *Reason #4: Present mortgages are low*

It is true that mortgages today are as low as they have ever been. Do you have good credit and 20% down? You could walk into a bank and walk out of it with a 30-year fixed mortgage with an interest rate of 5%. Is it smart to just buy because mortgages are low? It is not, and mortgage rates are already showing a steady climb. Only buy because you are ready to buy a house, not because the mortgage rates are great.

Assuming that you now have a good understanding of why you are buying a home, next, we will be discussing some important points you need to be aware of when making the home purchase decision.

CONSIDERATIONS YOU SHOULD HAVE BEFORE YOU BUY A HOME

Here is something you need to understand about buying a home; being too hasty when buying your house could turn bad for you.

Perhaps the biggest mistake you can make as a new home buyer is to rush in, set up the buying process and close the deal without thoroughly considering if it is the ideal kind of home for you. When this happens; and it is true that some buyers actually go ahead and do this, perhaps due to overexcitement or just buying a house for all the wrong reasons; there is often a very high likelihood that the house will become a burden as time goes by.

The house could end up being too big for you, leading to unnecessary space and house costs. The house could be in the wrong part of town, overly complicating such aspects of your life as your job and your kids' schooling. You could settle on what seems to be a great deal, only to discover the home is in an area prone to multiple burglaries, or is too close to, say, train tracks that make it impossible to sleep when trains roll over them at night.

Simply put, the unsavory situations you could put yourself into by rushing and buying a house without thinking matters through are limitless. Before you set up a meet with a seller, or have your buyer specialist do it for you; before you make a trip to conduct a house inspection, it is recommended that you make some thorough considerations on the house you want to buy.

This chapter will walk you through what you need to do to ensure that you streamline your options so that you are only left with the most ideal of them.

- **Consideration #1: What kind of home suits your needs best?**

This one has to be the very first consideration. You may already know this, but you have multiple options when it comes to buying residential property. You can opt for a traditional single-family home; the kind with a neat lawn and small picket fence. You could opt for a condo, a townhouse, a co-op (housing cooperative) or even a multi-family house with several units in it. The choice is really up to you.

However, consider that every option has its pros and cons. A traditional single-family home will be great for you if you want privacy, but it might cost way more than an apartment with similar space measurements. A multi- family house may be a lot easier on the purse, but you may be deprived of complete privacy compared to a traditional 1 unit home.

Ask yourself what your home ownership goals are. State them clearly and then make a decision on what property kind will assist you reach these goals. One of the unwritten rules of home ownership is this: A house or property will only make sense to the buyer if it helps him or her fulfill home ownership goals. A massive house that drains your bank account more than is necessary at the end of the month, or an undersized house that crams your sizable family into spaces that are too small are examples of homes that do not fulfill your home ownership goals.

(Here is a tip for you: Sometimes, the kind of home that will completely fulfill your home ownership goals will be a bit out of your price range. If you insist on purchasing this kind of home, there is an avenue you can follow. If you have the stomach for it, you stand to save a considerable amount of money in purchase fees by choosing a fixer-upper (basically a home that is not in great condition, which you then rehabilitate until it matches your ideal home image). However, understand that the amount of time, money and sweat equity required to turn a fixer-upper into a true home may end up being much more than you are willing to chew on.)

- **Consideration #2: Location is very important**

This is something you may already comprehend. Nevertheless, it is here so that it is re-emphasized for you.

Location is incredibly important. Wherever you live, you will be commuting from that particular place to your place of work. Unless you are the kind that hops onto free rides to work every day, you will spend money on your commute. You will also spend time here, which may prove to be even more costly than the money you spend. Both of these costs will be repeated over and over again, at least as long as you hold that job.

If you live close to your area of work, this is great: you can walk there or jump onto your bicycle, which will mean that your commuting costs hover around the zero mark. This is the ideal that you should be seeking, although it is not always possible to get.

- **Consideration #3: A 15-year mortgage will virtually always be a smarter idea than a 30-year mortgage**

The logic behind this consideration is simple: over the course of a 15-year mortgage, you will only end up paying about 1/3 of the interest that you would have paid over the course of a typical 30-year mortgage, to your bank. This is because not only is 15 years a much shorter time than 30 years, it will also come with lower interest rates. Having to pay three times more is a big deal, even if you have 15 extra years to distribute the monetary load.

Let us examine something relative to all this: if this tip is true and that you will indeed be paying about 3 times more with a 30-year mortgage, why is it that lots of people go for the 30-year mortgage anyway? The answer is quite simple: 30-year mortgages have lower monthly payment amounts. Even though it really is a poor strategy for the long-term, people will often look at the larger 15-year monthly payment amount and immediately recoil, believing that there is no way they will be able to afford it throughout the next 15 years.

Here is the truth for you though: If you are scared on the 15-year mortgage's monthly payment, understand that a 30-year mortgage for your home is an even worse option to have. Why is this? It is because you are buying more house than you can afford.

Unless you have a very unusual and compelling reason to prefer a 30-year mortgage, get a 15-year mortgage. If it looks like you cannot afford the payments on the 15-year mortgage, then you perhaps need to be looking at property that is more modestly priced.

- **Consideration #4: Never go above using 28% of the pay amount you take home as debt payments**

This is a great rule-of-thumb, at least as far as keeping your financial sanity goes.

Here is what to do: Take all your monthly debt payments for all your pre- existing debts and add them to your monthly mortgage payments (for a 15- year mortgage, not a 30-year mortgage.) If it all adds up to over 28% of your take-home monthly pay, then you are effectively dooming yourself to walking a thin financial tightrope. It will be wise to reconsider buying this home.

Understand that this is not some rule that is peddled around money circles. It is just something that we are recommending to you. At the very least, it will be effective in keeping you away from constant financial headaches and constant worry on what you can afford.

- **Consideration #5: Area crime rates are very important to consider before buying**

If you view a superb house that is going for a bargain price, it could well be that it is situated in an area that is high in crime. Thus, before you get way too involved in the buying process to back down (which basically means getting to

the stage where you are signing papers), check out the crime statistics of the area. Most of this information is online anyway, such as on websites such as www.mylocalcrime.com, meaning that you will not have to visit local police stations and then pore over their nondescript crime reports. Sites like www.mylocalcrime.com will provide snapshots of recent crime activity that has been reported in the vicinity of that home that you are considering buying.

However, do not be surprised if you see a lot more crime than you expect, especially if most of it involves petty crime. With such crimes as theft, pick- pocketing and the like, it may mean that the neighborhood is extremely vigilant in reporting them, meaning that there is something being done to reduce them.

- **Consideration #6: Walkability is a great thing to consider**

This one builds on the previous consideration. People love to be able to walk someplace, at least from time to time. That's not all; sidewalks encourage people to go out and explore the neighborhood, something that is vital in discouraging crime. Therefore, one thing you need to look out for is the presence of neighborhood sidewalks.

Granted, many newer housing developments will not have sidewalks but most neighborhoods that were developed before the 70s will have them.

- **Consideration #7: Neighborhood character is vital**

What is the neighborhood you are considering moving into like? This is an important question that you should seek answers for before you get serious about a prospective home. If you prefer quiet evenings with coffee and a good book and the neighbors like to have loud parties that start on Thursday and end on Sunday, it may be in your best interests to keep looking. And if you like to partying, but your neighbors sleep by 9pm every day, fitting in may be difficult for you.

Therefore, make sure to visit the neighborhood at different time periods every day. Visit at night too, so that you get a complete picture of what the neighborhood is like. If it is possible, meet some neighbors and talk to them; ask them about the neighborhood, the living patterns and what most of the people there are like. Make easy conversation and keep it light hearted. This will help you discern the neighborhood's character.

- **Consideration #8: Desist from buying the best house on the block**

It is often a lot better to purchase the worst property on the neighborhood than the best one of the lot. The worst can only appreciate in value while the best is as good as it can get. If you purchase the worst house, you could improve it and rehabilitate its facilities and in so doing, add its value as well as the overall value of what you have discerned to be a great neighborhood. Therefore, think about this when you go house shopping.

With everything we've learned so far in mind, I believe you now are ready to go to the next step after considering all the factors above. Next, we will be discussing about finances, with respect to home ownership.

BEING ABLE TO AFFORD YOUR NEW HOME

Pre-Approval Loan Programs And Why They Make Sense For The New Buyer

Let us cover pre-approval loan programs briefly. More and more people are going for pre-approval loan programs. What does it mean? Simply put, a pre-approval loan program implies pursuing and obtaining approval for a loan before you have lined up a specific property for purchase. You are applying for a loan and obtaining one without having marked some property or other out for buying, which automatically means that rather than determine the price you are willing to go for, and then applying for a loan that covers that amount, you will apply for whatever loan is in your reach and then determine the kind of home you will buy going by that loan amount.

It is a bit unconventional but upon closer inspection; you begin to see why it makes sense to go this way. Here are the top reasons why a pre-approval loan program might just be the way for you to go:

- ***Reason #1: You minimize the trauma of not knowing whether you qualify for a loan***

Picture this: You follow every directive in this book to the letter. You do everything you can to get the most ideal home possible, including hiring the best home buyer specialist. You go out of your way to be present for every home inspection and when all is said and done, you believe you have found the best property possible: there is a sizable playing field where Junior can play after school and the view from your bedroom window is stunning. Your vigilance in looking for the most suitable property has ensured that the price makes sense; you think you can afford it. However, upon getting to the bank, they pull up a late payment you made years earlier but forgot to repair, and it has damaged your credit. The bank refuses to loan you the exact amount you want. Can you see the frustration that would come up? It is much better to learn if you qualify or not, and then work from there.

- ***Reason #2: Once qualified, you look at the right priced homes***

This is a great perk, in all honesty. With this in place, you already know which homes you can afford and which ones you cannot afford. Regardless of how appealing property seems to you, it will be easier to resist the temptation of stretching yourself financially if it falls outside of your means.

- ***Reason #3: You will save money dealing with a comfortable seller***

This one stems from reason #2 more than anything else. The fact that you know exactly what you can afford means that you only approach sellers who value their property within your price range. This will create a good level of comfort from the start, since none of you is shifty about the pricing and when everything is cleared up, you will have saved a considerable amount of money.

- ***Reason #4: A pre-qualified buyer is a stronger bidder. You will close quicker***

You will be a lot more convincing to the seller if you are able to say, "I do not have to go to the bank to take out a loan, since I have already done that and have the money available." When you are able to say this, then you are automatically a serious buyer in the seller's eyes.

Loan preapproval seems to be a great thing that every home

buyer MUST pursue before doing anything. The question is; what exactly do you need to do to be approved? Let's discuss that next.

WHAT YOU NEED TO HAVE IN PLACE SO AS TO GET APPROVED FOR A MORTGAGE

What does it take to be able to take out a home mortgage? Sure enough, you need a good credit score, at the very least. In this chapter however, we will look at what else you need before you can apply for a home loan. Often times, your package has to include a salaried job and a history of reliable income that is verifiable by at least 2 years' worth of tax returns. Let's take this further:

Financial Requirements For A Mortgage Approval:

- *Great credit*

No matter how fresh you are with regard to home buying, this should not come as a surprise. Your credit score is one of the most critical factors that lenders will put into consideration whenever approving your mortgage application. The truth is; although your mortgage application may be approved even if your credit score is in the 600s-range, a score of 720+ will enable you get the best rates and will quite literally save you tens of thousands of dollars over your pay period (higher credit scores will mean lower interest rates attached. This is how you will actually be able to save tens of thousands of dollars.)

- *Down payment amount (money down)*

In years gone by, you could take out a mortgage/loan and not have to worry about down payment, since it was not always required. Those days are no longer with us and, if anything, you are much smarter than that anyway. The smart way to go about a home purchase is to do it "your grandfather's way": put at least 20% down and build on from there. In truth, your local bank may be willing to let you put down as little as 3.5% down, especially if your credit score is great. However, when you consider the amounts of money you will need to pay towards private mortgage insurance, you should be able to see just why it is best to wait until you can raise up a bigger own payment.

- *Cash-on-hand*

Besides having a down payment to put down, your local bank will want to see that buying a home will not drain your bank account. And, when all is said and done, it is good form to have something of an emergency fund, after all the closing and moving expenses are paid. It is a lot likelier that you will need them, than it is not.

- *Solid employment*

This is the 2nd most important factor, after a good credit score. The longer you have been working at your job, the better it is for you. If you are self- employed, this is well and good but nonetheless, prepare for a small battle before your mortgage gets approved. Most lenders will insist on seeing your tax returns for the last 2 or more years and will also calculate your income as the average of your income for the last 2 years. This could reduce the amount of financing that you qualify for.

With what we've discussed in mind, let's now discuss how you can save for your down payment for your first home.

How Do You Save For A Down Payment On Your Very First House?

As we have seen, when buying a house, offering a sizable down payment can save you lots of money, at least in the long run. This part shows you how to save up for a down payment. It shows you how to go about it the smart way.

Even if it is not in your plans to buy property right away, you are reading this book because you intend to do it at some point. Unlike saving up for, say, your retirement package, where the funds you put away will likely not be accessible for very many years, a down payment is a sizable amount of money that you will need to access soon.

This means that activities such as putting away small amounts of money and channeling them into the stock market will not work.

Here are 5 steps that will cover just how to start saving for probably your life's biggest purchase, and how to go about it in the smartest way possible:

Step #1: First, figure out how much you need to put down in savings

Before you anything else, figure out how much you need to save up. Set up a sit-down with a mortgage lender (or your local bank), who will inform you the mortgage amount you qualify for.

Speaking generally though, it will be unwise to exceed 28% of your stable monthly income on house expense. (In truth, 40% should be the absolute limit, but it is much smarter to keep it under 28%. You stand to have less financial headaches anyway.) If your income is $5,000, you can safely allocate

$1,400- $1,500 a month to your future down payment.

The $1,400/$1,500 will be inclusive of the mortgage principal plus interest, real estate taxes, PMI (private mortgage insurance) and HOA (homeowners association) rates.

With present mortgage rates going at around 4.5%, this will translate to an amount of $177,500.

So as to arrive at the amount of money that you can afford to put up to pay for your house, you will have to take this $177,500 and add the down payment on top of it. Remember we said 20% is the ideal down payment to make (and today's tight-fisted lending market tends to mostly insist on it, anyway). You can definitely put down less but this is often at the expense of paying a higher rate. And if you have credit issues, it may well be that you will be getting no mortgage at all.

Staying consistent with our example of $177,500 and making a 20% down payment provision, let us calculate our down payment dollar amount:

$177,500/ 0.80 = $221,875

$221,875 - $177,500 = $44,375 (Rounded off to $45,000)

Thus, you will be purchasing a $222,000 house with $177,500 mortgage with a down payment of roughly $45,000.

(PS: You do not have to get hang up with all these calculations; your mortgage lender will do them for you anyway. However, it does not hurt to be aware of what they consist of.)

Step #2: Determine what your timeframe is

This one is also important. If you plan on buying a home in 5 years' time, then going by our example in step #1, you should be prepared to save up $9,000 every year ($45,000/ 5 = $9,000).

As you would expect, the shorter the timeframe, the higher you can expect your annual savings to be.

Step #3: Find the absolute best way to save for your down payment

As a clear cut rule, seeing as the money you are putting down for the down payment of your house has a defined purpose attached to it, and needs to be arrived at within a specific timeframe, it will be very unwise to save it up in risky investment vehicles (think stocks, bonds, real estate investment trusts etc). It will be downright silly to think of gambling with it, to see if it multiplies. Rather, the only options should be risk-free investment vehicles, such as standard old-fashioned savings accounts or a certificate of deposit.

Sure enough, you may be able to make more by going the way of risky-type vehicles of investment, but there is a very real possibility that you might lose your money as well.

Understand this: if you are saving for your future house, the worst case scenario is not missing out on returns- it is losing money meant to buy a house, and losing out on the house.

Step #4: Find room in your budget...or make some if there is none to be found

We are talking about saving up thousands of dollars every year here. You will have to find a way to either make the same money you make do more for you by doing such things as cutting back on expenses, or find an additional gig to supplement to your income. Sometimes, you may have to do both.

The thing is, you have to find a way to make room in your budget so that you are able to save the kind of money that you need to make a down payment. And in truth, being able to do this will prepare you adequately for the management of the tighter budget that ownership of a home comes with.

Step #5: Set up an automated savings plan

Unless it is in your nature to save, something that most of us cannot boast of being, you may need to automate the savings process. This may mean some payroll savings plan, or something along those lines. Just like you do with your 401 (k) savings plan, you should allocate some percentage or some dollar amount of your monthly pay directly into a savings account or money market account.

The beauty of this is that not only is the process automatic, it is also invisible. You will not see it happen, but every month, money will leave your paycheck to your preferred savings account. This will eliminate the temptation (as well as ability) to spend this money on other more immediate purposes.

With what we've discussed so far in mind, let's now talk about mortgages i.e. what different mortgage rates mean as well as how to get a mortgage for your home.

THE MORTGAGE QUESTION: THE INS & OUTS OF MORTGAGE FINANCING

Before we discuss the hows of mortgage, let's start by building an understanding of mortgage rates.

A Brief Explanation on Mortgage Rates

A full examination and explanation of mortgage rates would not only go on for too long, but you would likely only be more confused at the end of the lesson. As such, this section will keep it simple. We will examine, briefly, the differences between fixed and adjustable-rate mortgages. We will also look at mortgage points. It is often quite a task to be clear and simple when explaining mortgage rates- even your local bank will tend to put knots in your brain a lot of the time- but we have done a job in making everything here as simple, clear and straightforward as possible.

The Difference between the Adjustable-Rate Mortgage & Fixed-Rate Mortgage

Let's start with Fixed rate mortgage.

A fixed rate mortgage works exactly like it sounds- regardless of whether the interest rates go up or down, or simply plateau, the fixed mortgage rate will remain the same for as long as you pay down your loan.

Conversely, an adjustable rate mortgage has the capacity to go up or down (though it will mostly go up, which is easy to understand if you comprehend how lending institutions and money in general works.) The climbs and falls of the rate will be dependent on the overall rates of interest throughout the market.

Sometimes, it will be possible to get an adjustable rate mortgage at an interest rate that is much lower than what you can get with a fixed rate one, but the rate may well shoot past that of the fixed rate mortgage in a few years. Thus, if you decide on a favorable looking adjustable interest rate, you at least know what you are getting.

ARMs

Other rate mortgages that are variable (known these days as adjustable rate mortgages or ARMs) include a super low introductory mortgage rate for 5 or 7 years, followed thereafter by a much higher rate. This sort of loan is designed for the home buyer who expects to live in his or her home for a very short time period before either refinancing at a later time, or flipping the home for a buck.

There is nothing wrong with adjustable mortgage rates, and it is not the job of this book to bash them like so many others do. If you know what you are doing and your finances resemble those of a responsible adult, feel free to make them an option. However, in some situations, they can be extremely dangerous and to be honest, they played a very big role in the massive amount of foreclosures and real estate price collapses in the 2008 recession.

What Are Mortgage Points?

Mortgage points, essentially, are fees that you pay on a mortgage loan when the loan is distributed. A point is equal to 1% of mortgage value. Taking the example of a $200,000 mortgage, a point equals $2,000.

Why would you pay mortgage points? This is a good question. In many situations, if the borrower has an underwhelming credit score or the lending is really tight, a home buyer may resort to paying points so as to be able to get any mortgage loan at all.

Often times, however, the mortgage lender will offer the option of paying points in exchange for a lower rate of interest on your mortgage. This is mostly how mortgage points are utilized.

With what we have discussed so far in mind, let's now talk about how to go about shopping for a home loan.

Shopping For A Mortgage: Steps To Finding Your Perfect Home Loan

That is right; shopping for a mortgage is indeed a thing. You do not just settle on the first mortgage that the lender throws at you, if you want the best deal. The problem is, most new home buyers make this very mistake, and it is often an expensive one.

When you go about buying your home, make a point of not just shopping for the home but for the mortgage as well. The right mortgage is just as important as the right house. After all, you will be stuck with it for years, making a payment every month that passes. For better or for worse, the interest rate that you allow yourself to get locked in will impact your financial future.

What is this book's advice? Consider all options, as far as mortgage loans applications go, and make a decision after you have examined them all. Here is a guide for you, to help you as you shop for a mortgage:

Item #1: The Mortgage Application Stages

1: Prequalification:

Before you even go out shopping for a house, consider getting a prequalification letter for your mortgage. Note that this is different from pre- approval, and getting a "prequal" does not mean you are approved. Simply call a bank and answer the questions they ask you about your income, assets gained and debts in place. They will also ask after the kind of house you are looking at. The bank will then write you a letter informing any prospective sellers, as well as your buyer specialist, that you are in a position to afford a mortgage that runs up to a certain amount. A prequalification letter does not mean too much in the scheme of things, but it is a great tool for easing off sellers' fears that the financing may not be available even if they accept your offer.

2: Pre-approval:

We covered this a few chapters ago. You will be required to submit an application for a mortgage and the bank will then evaluate your credit as well as carry some research on the home you want to buy (if you already have one lined up). If everything is in order, they will agree to finance the home, and you can then move on towards closing the deal. Otherwise, if you do not have a house lined up, you can continue searching for one, but this time with absolute confidence that you can indeed close.

2: Closing:

This is where everything comes together. If everything is in order, the mortgage will get finalized and you will make the step from being a home buyer to a home owner. This book will cover the closing bit later on.

Item #2: Type Of Loan

There are 4 common institutional mortgage loan types: conventional, FHA, VA and jumbo. Your very first step, with regard to these loan types, will be researching what loan type you qualify for. You should also determine which loan type will be best for your specific situation. Each loan type will have its drawbacks and benefits.

VHA loans:

These are guaranteed by the Department of Veteran Affairs. They require as little as no down payment, but then again, they are only available to qualified veterans.

FHA loans:

They are backed by the Federal Housing Administration. They require as low as 3.5% down. They can be very helpful, especially if your cash reserve is limited but the drawback here is that with less than 20% down, you can expect to pay monthly PMI, private mortgage insurance, which is often lofty.

Conventional loans

You will have to put up at least 20% down payment. There will be no PMI required. This is your best bet but then again, your finances have to be reasonably in order.

Jumbo mortgage

They must be in use if you are "financing considerably more than conventional loan limits allow." In most parts of the US, the limit sits at an interesting

$417,000 (at least as from 2010). Why they didn't make it a flat $400,000 or even $420,000 is only known to them. These loans usually have some special restrictions as well as special credit requirements.

Item #3: Terms of repayment

When you are choosing among the various home loan types, you will also need to consider the terms of repayment. Basically, what we are pointing to here is your choice between a fixed rate mortgage and an adjustable rate mortgage. We have already discussed the differences between both, as well as additional content on mortgage points in this very part of the book.

Item #4: Rates Of Interest

Getting the very best interest rate possible is an important bit when it comes to getting an affordable mortgage.

Before you call mortgage lenders, scour the internet for the latest mortgage interest rates. Any reputable bank will have a website and this website will be regularly updated to show the latest rates. At least this way, you will know what to expect before you place your call. If the national interest rate is at, say, 4.4% at noon and a lender offers 5%, you understand that you have room to negotiate and bring the rate down. The closer the lender sits to the daily national average, the less profit he or she is taking and the sweeter the deal is for you.

3 lenders should be your absolute minimum: get quotes from all of them and compare their rates on the same loan type.

Item #5: Locking In Your Rate

Once you have settled on a mortgage that you like, and receive your pre- approval, ask your lender to lock in your interest rate. Do not just stop here though: ask the lender to provide you with a written document that states the particular interest rate that you locked in and the amount of mortgage points you need to pay (if this is part of the package). Ensure the document also states the period of time the interest rate will be locked in before the present offer expires.

Locking in the interest rate is important: it means that even if interest rates rise within the time period you were guaranteed, you will not be compelled to pay a higher interest rate, and can continue paying your lower rate.

Having discussed about mortgages comprehensively, you should now be able to check all boxes as far as shopping for the best deal for financing your home purchase is concerned.

Let's now move on to discussing about searching for a property to purchase.

The Home Searching Process

You can use different approaches to find properties to purchase. But before you make a move, it is important to work with a buyer specialist. Let's discuss that in detail.

Using A Buyer Specialist

Who/What Is A Buyer Specialist?

Let us keep this simple.

A buyer specialist, also referred to as a buyer representative or buyer rep, is someone or some party that a house buyer enlists with to represent his or her interests in the process of finding an appropriate home or property. The buyer specialist acts as a buffer; rather than the buyer having to put in the miles, blindly seeking out property and risking paying a bloated price, or having to settle for a subpar property, the buyer specialist does all of the legwork for him or her. The buyer specialist will hunt for the best possible property, at least going by your list of preferences, ensure that you pay the best possible price for the property and walk you through the entire process as it unfolds.

A buyer specialist is a bit like a godfather (at least a proper buyer specialist is) when it comes to house hunting, except that you pay for the service.

As a first time home buyer, it makes all the sense in the world to seek out the services of a buyer specialist. Not only will you no longer act blindly, leaving important elements to chance, you will be able to close faster and learn a thing or two via constant consultations with him or her.

I know you might be wondering; what benefits will a buyer specialist bring to the table? Let's discuss that:

Why Working With A Buyer Specialist Is Important

Besides helping the home hunting process go along in a speedier fashion, and bringing some experience to the table, what are the benefits of using a proper buyer specialist? Understand that this is not some aloof, detached real estate agent we are talking about here- anybody who describes themselves as "buyer specialist" has to pledge to be more than just a connector between buyer and seller.

A buyer specialist, more than anything else, is your "personal shopper." In addition to helping you find the right home, he or she is obligated to look out for you. Just like a lawyer represents you in his capacity, so does a buyer specialist in his own capacity.

Here are the benefits a buyer specialist brings to the table:

#1: Loyalty

The buyer specialist must be different from the conventional real estate agent. He or she must always work in your best interests. The buyer specialist is a lot more thorough with the house shopping. If there are crucial elements amiss, then no matter how good the deal looks, he or she will walk away for your sake.

#2: Disclosure

With a buyer specialist, you are not simply another piece on the business chessboard. The relationship has a personalized touch to it. The buyer specialist will ensure that you know every relevant thing regarding your desired property, as well as all the processes involved. He or she makes a point to consult regularly with you, no matter how green you are on house matters.

#3: Confidentiality

The buyer specialist will protect your information with his or her life. Your situation and details are not to be spread around, or used as an example, unless you consent to it.

#4: Due skill and care

We are talking about the negotiation process here. The buyer specialist will drain as much skill and wisdom as is at his or her disposal into getting you the best possible deal. He or she will also ensure everything moves on in a timely manner.

The next question you may have is:

What Should The Ideal Buyer Specialist Do For You?

Using a buyer specialist is a smart move in that it makes it easier to not just find property in your price range, but great property that presents value for money. A buyer specialist, in a way, plays the role a baby walker plays to a baby; they help you get to the point you want to get to, without stumbling or overcompensation, which would have otherwise been impossible without their assistance. However, the market is full of people who call themselves buyer specialists but who are no more than posers. How do you determine a buyer specialist is genuine and will actually do the job for you? You start by asking what to expect from them, then sit back and judge their replies using the following checklist:

#1: The ideal buyer specialist will exclusively represent your interests as a homebuyer

This should always be at the top of the pile. A buyer specialist with professionalism and experience understands that your home is yours, and not theirs. As such, your preferences and choices reign supreme. It could be that the buyer specialist believes that some home you passed over actually fits your needs better but he or she is obligated to first suggest to you that property A is actually better than B before doing anything else. And even then, they must listen to what you have to say and accept your choice as law. He or she must not override you, or keep insisting on going one way when you want to go a different way. This is poor form, and a proper buyer specialist will understand this. A buyer specialist is there to represent your interests, not his or her own, or somebody else's who may have promised to pay some sort of commission.

#2: Keep your financial information and price intentions confidential

In short, the buyer specialist has to treat your information with the utmost respect. And there is no greater measure of respect, at least as far as information goes, than confidentiality. Your financial information must only be known by you and the buyer specialist. Your price intentions, however frustrating or even bloated they are, must be kept secret. You are not there to be used as an example. It does not matter if you are in the vicinity or not; the buyer specialist cannot go off spouting things like, "And by the way I have this client who wants such and such kind of house but is being unrealistic about the pricing." On top of helping you look for a house, it is also the buyer specialist's business to keep his mouth shut.

#3: Counsel with you as often as possible regarding the property type and location that will meet your needs

As we said in point #1, your choices and preferences reign supreme and they are law to the buyer specialist. This is why he or she needs to get as personal with you as possible regarding what you want. It should not be enough to the buyer specialist that a certain property in a certain location "fits your needs approximately." He or she has to do everything possible to find the best property for you. They need to call and liaise with you often and make sure all the specifics are met. In this capacity, the buyer specialist acts more like a concerned friend. And while the level of professionalism must never drop, the formal attitude should be gradually replaced with a more relaxed, informal one. The buyer specialist must see you as a person first; one whose needs need to be addressed seriously, and then as an opportunity to do business.

#4: Diligently search for the ideal property for you

This goes hand in hand with point #3. The buyer specialist consults heavily with you and then goes to work looking for the very best deal. And it shouldn't just be a price thing- every bit in the package has to be considered. Do you want property closer or further away from the highway? Do you insist on being only so far from the local school, on account of your kids? It is ideal; of course, that as little time as possible is spent on the property hunting, but a thorough job of it has to be done nonetheless.

#5: Point out the strengths and weaknesses of various properties

We said that your preferences and choices reign supreme and this remains true all the way. The ideal situation is that you get what you want and then the buyer specialist can call it a day. However, it is also the buyer specialist's job to furnish you with the truth at all points. He or she needs to point out the strengths and weaknesses of all prospective properties, even though the result of the advice is a prolonged house hunt. The buyer specialist ought to only be satisfied with the best property for you. He/she does not tell you what to do, but points out facts and allows you to make your decisions like an adult.

#6: Negotiate exclusively on your behalf as the home buyer; and only settle on the best purchase price, terms as well as other pertinent conditions

Naturally, the buyer specialist may be a lot savvier when it comes to property value estimation and haggling than you are. Beyond taking home their paycheck, they must insist that you get the property at the best possible price. This means that the buyer specialist must be willing to walk away, and thus hurt his or her earnings at least for that day, if he or she feels you are not getting the best deal possible.

#7: Offer an independent, professional written inspection of the property you choose and quality home warranty as part of the purchase price

The truth is that the majority of the buyer specialists out there fail to do any of these, especially the latter. A lot of those who actually do the former (written inspection) gloss over certain details so as to make a quick buck. The reason "independent" is part of the inspection description is because the buyer specialist needs to be as straightforward, unbiased and thorough as possible. If the carpeting in the property is disgusting and it is clear that the current owner refuses to potty train their dog, it should be part of the inspection report.

Now that you know what a buyer specialist is expected to do, you need to understand your place in the relationship between you and the buyer specialist. Let's get to that next.

What Can You Do To Assist Your Buyer Specialist Find The Most Ideal Home Property For You?

Now that you know who a buyer specialist is, and what he or she stands for, you likely understand that you will have to be a bit liberal with the information you give. One of the hallmarks of a great buyer specialist is the eagerness to consult often and glean as much as possible. This will be impossible to achieve if you do not go out of your way to bare your heart, at least as far as your prospective home goes. So what can you do to help your buyer specialist do their job to the best of their ability? How do you play your role perfectly, with regard to your buyer specialist? Here are some ideas:

#1: Review the listing information on those homes, which interest you/buyer specialist recommends you

Why is this necessary? For starters, you know what you want more than the buyer specialist does. When you review the homes, you will be able to tell which ones appeal to you the most and which ones you can pass over. The next step will be to forward your streamlined list of home options to your buyer specialist, making their job to find the best property for you easier.

#2: Tell your buyer specialist if and when you change your requirements and as such, need to see additional properties

You will be expecting promptness from your buyer specialist on all fronts. You should do the same, with regard to him or her. If you do change your property requirements due to one reason or the other, let your buyer specialist know there are changes and why you saw it fit to make them. This will enable the buyer specialist to save on time and look for a new set of properties, and not expend energy on looking for properties, which no longer interest you.

#3: Take accurate notes on and photographs of homes that interest you

For one, this involves you more in the house hunting process. The other thing is that such notes and photographs will arm your buyer specialist even better with regard to finding the best possible home for you. He or she will understand even better what you are looking for.

#4: Request that the buyer specialist show you all the homes you love in your price range

In a bid to only have the most ideal homes for you in the list, the buyer specialist may do too much "chopping" and in so doing, eliminate options that would otherwise have been very appealing to you. Insist on seeing everything you love: this will help you help your buyer specialist.

#5: Shop for a mortgage before you shop for a home

We have insisted on this time and time again up to this point. Make a point of getting a pre-approval before you even approach a buyer specialist. Why do this? With a pre-approval, you will know exactly how much you can spend. Better yet, you will be assured that you have the money once you settle on something. It would be in poor form on your part if you took up the buyer specialist's time and energy to get you a great deal, only to discover you are ineligible for a mortgage.

Now that you understand how to work with a buyer specialist, let's now look into a checklist you can follow to get your ideal home.

Using A Home Buying Checklist To Get Your Ideal Home

They say that part of being an adult is accepting some unappealing things and moving on with life. As a first time home buyer, you may be strapped for cash, or time, or some other resource that is crucial. As such, finding the right home for you may mean having to separate what you WANT from what you actually NEED.

Any competent buyer specialist will lead with 2 questions, when a prospective buyer comes in looking to shop for a house:

1. What is it that you want in the house?
2. With that out of the way, what is it that you need in the house?

Of course, to many people, the subtlety is absolutely lost on them. If a first time home buyer comes up to us and states her needs as being "a home at a cul-de-sac's end, with the master bedroom facing east so I wake up along with the rising sun", so be it: she is our client and we will do our best to give her what she needs.

Distinguishing Needs From Wants

But let us be a little honest here: You NEED a good roof protecting you, clean water that runs constantly, enough heat for the winter days and perhaps air conditioning, if the weather is often hot. But when it comes to such things as pools, white picket fences and 2.5 bathrooms? Well, you do not need these things so much as you want to have them.

It is part of our job to furnish you with valuable advice, so here is some: starting from this moment, you should be ready to distinguish your wants from your needs so that when the time comes, you are 100% confident on the kinds of homes you would like to table offers for.

Here is how:

#1: Envision your dream home and start from there

Visualize your dream home. What does it look like? Is it on some mammoth land plot, with enough space to exhaust every pet you have ever wanted to own? Is it some condo on the 60th floor, overlooking the night lights? Where is its location? Think about other things that make it special to you.

By this point, you know what a pre-approval is and why it makes sense to have one before you even go house shopping. With a pre-approval in hand, you know what you can afford and what you cannot. With your price in mind, you may well need to forego some of your wants. Are you unsure of what is reasonable and what does not fit in your price range? This is where a competent buyer specialist comes in. The buyer specialist's job involved being familiar with the area, understanding what various homes will going for and know how much added features, such as additional bedrooms or swimming pools will add to the price.

#2: Now work backwards from there

As you piece the vision of your dream home together, you may discover that there are some features that you are unwilling to sacrifice, or are willing to pay more to have. It could be that you want to live 20 minutes away from work; it could be that you have always lived in places with open kitchens and could not imagine yourself in a home without one; it could be that a family member is disabled, and you insist on having wheelchair access for him or her. Such things sit closer to needs than wants.

However, it is sometimes easy to pick out your wants among the needs. For example, you may say something like, "You know, an indoor Jacuzzi would be a wondrous thing, would it not?" Here is one way to look at all this: wants are those things that you can either add or change on your own.

For instance, you may be a massive Raiders fan and would love a house with silver knobs, handles and other surfaces, and black carpeting to top it all off. Obviously, and with very little effort too, you can make all your desired changes. There are people who will refuse to consider getting their hands dirty and putting some work on the home themselves. You may be part of this group, perhaps out of habit. However, this is the truth: when you are flexible with your wants, it becomes infinitely easier to find great homes at great prices. The reason so many couples on those televised house hunting shows cannot seem to get a fitting house, despite having dozens of options to choose from, is because they have little flexibility on their wants.

#3: Keep your focus on the value items

In real estate, value items "are features that add value to the property, to future buyers."

As you evaluate your needs and your wants, it is a smart idea to consider value items more than you do those items you have a personal preference for, but fail to add considerable value.

Here are some items that qualify as value items:

- Dual pane windows
- Hardwood floors
- Granite countertops
- Beautiful landscaping
- Land
- Being in, say, a highly rated school district

A great buyer specialist will be able to aid you in determining subtle differences between valuable features and features whose only value lies in your bias toward them.

With this said, certainly some big features do not always add value. For instance; does a pool automatically add value? Yes? How about no?

The thing with pools is that a lot of buyers who want houses with pools are never willing to pay much for them. In some areas, having a pool may even qualify as a negative to a prospective buyer. Then you have those people who just do not like them at all- they could have a personal loathing of swimming as an activity or they have young children and are scared of the risks involved.

Having all we've discussed in mind, lets now look at the process of buying a home.

THE HOME BUYING PROCESS: A HOW TO GUIDE

Before we discuss the steps you should take in the home purchase process, assuming that your home search was successful, let's discuss some things you need to be aware of about homes and the home buying process that many buyers don't take into consideration until it is too late.

Things You Should Know About Homes And Home Buying That Most Buyers Fail To Know

These are great tips that will serve you well not just in your first home buying process but in every other one you take part in, in the future. They are great strategies that will ensure that you settle on the best possible deals and stay away from common mistakes that many first time home buyers make.

#1: Always choose a home with an eye toward future needs

This is quite important to do. It is inevitable that you will change in the future, or at least your circumstances will. Buying a one bedroom condo at 28, when you intend to be married with a family at 30, is self-defeating, as you will be compelled to shop for fresh property in the near future. Remember that buying a home is very much an investment: if you can stretch yourself today to buy a home that you can grow into, in the future, then by all means do it.

#2: Once you are ready to buy, move with speed

It is an unwritten real estate law that the best properties go fast. Once you and your buyer specialist have made a decision to buy a certain home, be prepared to make any relative decisions quickly. If the property is 40 minutes away from your work place when you fancied one only 20 minutes away, make a quick decision to either resign yourself to waking up 20-30 minutes earlier every day, or move on and look for something else. If you find the right home today but are only willing to buy it tomorrow, you may already be too late by the time tomorrow rolls around. Of course, we are only being figurative here, but you get the point.

#3: Not every fixer-upper presents a good deal

Fixer-uppers can present some tasty deals but not all of them do. Some of them may seem like great deals but once you evaluate the rehabilitation costs necessary, discover that you will need to invest far too much. Consult with your buyer specialist and a seasoned rehabilitation pro if you have to, if you do consider settling for a fixer-upper.

#5: Shop with your head and not with your heart

It is 100% true what you have heard- home shopping is often more emotional than rational for most people. It will help you greatly to step in with a cold, emotionless attitude once you decide to get shopping. Critique everything and be unwilling to accept negatives in property, unless the positives absolutely outweigh them. The heart tends to cost people money- use your head when you house shop.

#6: Location is extremely vital

No home is an island, unless you are literally home shopping for single homes in islands. Not only does the neighborhood determine, to some extent, the overall quality of your life there, but the very value of your home will be defined by the homes that surround it. Buying what seems to be an absolute peach of a home right in the middle of a slew of abandoned homes and broken down fences will make it very hard to sell it off at a profit later, if you decide to move.

Now that you are well informed before you make the decision to actually commit to buy a certain home, let me discuss some eye opening secrets about the home purchase process that will save you a lot of trouble.

The 5 Best Kept Secrets With Regard To Home Buying

This is coverage on some things you ought to do just before you go about buying a home, or if you are aiming to buy one in a matter of months. They are not exactly considerations that you ought to make- you NEED to do take care of everything addressed here so that you ensure that your home buying and ownership processes face as little turbulence as possible.

#1: Keep your money exactly where it is

You will be wise to apply this one if you are 6 months away or less from buying your home. It is not smart at all to make some big purchases or move your money around in this time period. Why is this? Think about this: why would you want to take a chance with your credit profile a short time before you apply for your mortgage? The lender will insist on seeing that you are a reliable borrower. They will want a paper trail to enable you to get the best possible loan that they can give you. Opening new credit cards, amassing debt or splurging on costly items just before you apply for your mortgage is self-defeating, and you will be making it difficult for the lender to let you borrow money.

#2: Avoid border disputes by all means

We place sufficient stress on carrying out a proper home inspection in this book. Well, you must not limit home inspection to the inside of the house- it is absolutely essential that you have your buyer specialist have a survey carried out on your property. This way, you know exactly what you are purchasing. When you know exactly where your property lines are, it may save you an unnecessary tiff with your neighbors, and money in terms of legal fees.

#3: It is foolhardy to try and "time the market"

It is pointless to try and time the housing market. Trying to do so is a bit like trying to anticipate when a goal will be scored in a professional soccer game. It is impossible and the only thing you will end up succeeding at is wasting your time and mental energy. The best time to dip into the market and buy a home is when you have enough funds to do it. It really is as simple as this.

#4: Look out for sleeper costs

They say the difference between renting and owning a home is the sleeper costs. Too many buyers will just focus on paying their mortgage and ignore everything else. You should be aware of- and budget for- other expenses such as utilities, property taxes and other homeowner associated dues. Be sure to budget for sleeper costs before you get to buying so that you do not risk losing your new home.

#5: Seeing as you are buying the house and not dating it, treat its purchase accordingly

If you purchase based on what your emotions are showing you, it is very likely that you will end up with a poor deal. Keep your eyes open and your head straight- this is how to guarantee you get the best possible deal.

Let's discuss the next thing; freehold vs. leasehold.

Do You Opt For Freehold Or Leasehold When Purchasing? A Look at Both and What You Can Expect From Them

This section will take an in depth look into both freehold and leasehold, with regard to buying a house. Do not be put off by the terminology- simply put, buying freehold simply means you buy the house as well as the property it sits on. You own the property as well as the land it is in. If you are purchasing a flat, you are purchasing leasehold, or purchasing into "a share of freehold". While you do own the flat, you by no means own the property it sits on outright. This guide will break down the ways that you may own property: buying freehold, buying leasehold or buying leasehold, with a share of the freehold.

What Is A Freehold?

Let us have a deeper look at what a freehold is. The buyer of the freehold, referred to as the freeholder, will own the property in a straightforward manner, with inclusion of the land that the house sits on. If you opt to purchase a freehold, then all the responsibilities that come with managing the house as well as the piece of land it sits on fall squarely on your shoulders. It is up to you to budget for all the costs that are involved.

If you are looking to buy a house outright, you are likely looking to buy a freehold. Are there perks that come with buying a freehold? You bet there are.

Perks of having a freehold/being a freeholder

The bulk of perks here lie in the "You do not have to" category. With a freehold, you do not have to:

- Have any worries over the lease running out. This cannot happen, since you own the property outright.

- Go through the freeholder (otherwise known as the landlord) when you want to make changes to the property, seeing as you are the freeholder

- Spend money on such things as service charges, rental

fees, or just about any other charge that a landlord will aim your way

In short, a freehold gives you 100% power over your property. The only thing you cannot do is pile up toxic waste material in your yard, or something else just as crazy, as the state will step in and penalize you. Owning a share of the freehold It is possible to purchase the freehold from your landlord, should you choose to buy a flat, along with other leaseholders who reside in the block of flats that you live in. You can do this, but at least 50% of the leaseholders have to agree to purchase a share. This is often a great strategy to employ if you opted to buy a flat rather than a house, as it gives you a lot more control of the home and by extension, the costs that you fork out, with regard to it.

Doing so will also enable you to easily extend your lease for up to, say, 999 years.

However, understand that it might prove to be expensive to purchase the freehold this way. It may also be a necessity to team up with the other leaseholders like you in setting up a company that will deal with the building's management. You can either do this or find an agent to do it for you at a fee.

What Is Leasehold?

With leasehold, you will own the home as well as the land it sits on for the length of time your lease agreement states. Of course, the lease agreement will be between you and the freeholder, landlord.

When the lease comes to an end, property ownership immediately reverts to the freeholder, unless the two of you agree to extend your lease.

Most of the mansionettes and flats you see are owned this way, at least in the US.

Purchasing Leasehold:

When you purchase leasehold, you take over the previous owner's lease.

Before you make your offer, there will be a few things to consider:

- Exactly how many years are left on the lease?
- How do you plan on budgeting for service costs as well as other relative costs?
- How much of an effect will the lease have on being able to get a mortgage?
- How will the lease affect the resale value of the property?

Just how vital is the lease length?

Let us look at a few things you ought to be familiar with, with regard to leasehold:

To put it simply, if your lease is less than seventy years, you may struggle to land a mortgage

The lender will usually insist that the lease run at least 25 years beyond the mortgage's end (which is what makes a lease that is less than 70 years not ideal a lot of the time).

As a result, it may also prove difficult to sell property on if the lease runs for less than 80 years. Think about this: if the new owner is looking for a 25-year mortgage, it will mean that the lease will have to run for 50+ years for the lender to consider the mortgage. If you have already gone through, say, 20-30 years of your 70 year lease, you can see why it may be difficult to convince a buyer to spend on it.)

If your intention is to sell off a leasehold you are purchasing, the first thing to ponder over is how long you intend to live out your lease, and just how many years will be left on it by that time

Charges To Expect With Leasehold

Charges will vary, going by particular property. However, you can expect to pay for:

- Repair as well as maintenance of exterior fence/walls
- Ground rent
- Administration charges
- Maintaining communal gardens
- Electricity bills, for communal areas
- Buildings insurance

There are many more charges that may be involved, especially service charges, which is why you should make a point of being aware of service charges involved before you buy leasehold.

Do You Opt For Freehold Or Leasehold?

Your financial situation is only known to you but if this book were to make a recommendation, the freehold is it. Freehold ownership is as simple and straightforward as it gets; just look at the brief coverage of it in this chapter alone, compared to the coverage that leasehold gets. However, there is no crime in buying leasehold- you just have to understand that there may be a lot more factors to consider.

A Step By Step Account On The Buying Process

At this point, you are armed with sufficient information to take the plunge. Let us now explore what to expect from the actual process of buying a home and going through potential deals. The first thing to know is that this is rarely ever a tranquil time. While your buyer specialist will do a great job in shielding you from the hassle and chaotic atmosphere of the home buying process, you will likely still experience the turbulence that comes with the whole thing. However, if you are prepared to handle it all (or at the very least, the paperwork that may pile up significantly), you will get through the process just fine and perhaps learning a few new things.

This is the basic sequence you can expect as a home buyer:

#1: *Look For And Find A Home*

This book has already covered a lot of ground with regard to house shopping. You understand that in order to get the best deal possible, it is necessary to put in more legwork and look at as many options as is possible. You now know that it is unwise to go for the best property among a bunch of lowly ones, as its appreciation will be almost impossible to achieve. You at least understand what wants and needs are, and that a willingness to be flexible with the former allows you to be able to find a good house a lot more easily.

One other thing we can add here is driving around the neighborhood looking for a good deal. Certainly, with this book's advocacy for buyer specialists, the activity of driving around looking for prospective property will be little more than a hobby. However, you never know what you can find by driving around and having a look at the more quietly advertised properties. You may find a gem that you would have never found otherwise. And if you do stumble on a gem that you think outperforms every other tabled option, do not, in a spate of eagerness, jump right in and begin talking to the seller's agent before contacting your buyer specialist first. It doesn't take too much thinking to see why it might not be a good idea to deal the seller's agent directly as a first time home buyer.

But what if you are on a tight budget that does not quite fit your ideal home? We covered the subject of wants and needs, and why it is important to be flexible with your wants. Sometimes, however, your preferences are completely reasonable but your local bank is only willing to lend you so much. What do you do? Well, you will need to look at properties whose full potential has not been realized yet. Relay this directive to your buyer specialist, so that he or she knows what to go for. You may well find a house that fits every one

of your specifications but has about the most hideous wallpaper you have ever seen, and the lawn looks like a small jungle. Go for it. At first, you will have to put up with the unsavory qualities it has but with time, you can make the appropriate changes and in so doing, have the house reach its full potential.

#2: Consider The Financing Options Available For You & Secure Financing

This one will be quite a read, so it will help if you follow closely. There is a lot to this one and if you are patient enough to pick up as much information as you can about it (which starts by reading the content here), you can make the financing process a lot freer of headaches. You stand to save some good money too, if you know what you are doing. Let us have a look at just what we mean:

1st time home buyers have a vast variety of options to aid them get into a home; more options than those available to other kinds of purchasers. The 1st time home buyer, if he or she sees it fit and has sufficient money anyway, can go for a typical Federal Housing Authority (FHA) backed mortgage. If the first time buyer is a little strapped for cash, there are special loan programs geared for the beginner. A lot of the latter will offer minimum down payments that go as low as 3%, versus the standard 20%, while some will require no down payment. However, recall that this book has insisted that putting up at least 20% down payment is your best bet, as you will avoid having to pay too much for the home later on in accumulated payments.

As a first time home buyer:

Use HUD's resource list (HUD & FHA have been covered in this book). The

FHA and the loan program it backs are part of the HUD's makeup.

Make a point to look to your IRA. Let us cover this a little more: The very first chapter of this book covers what a 1st time home buyer is, in a legal capacity. The IRA makes a point of using the descriptions we provided to determine if you qualify as a first time home buyer. With this out of the way, every person has a lifetime amount of $10,000, which may be withdrawn, entirely free of penalties, from his or her IRA. If you and your spouse are shopping for a house together, you could pitch in and withdraw a maximum amount of

$20,000 to put down for your first home. However, make a point of using the money within 4 months (the IRA puts it down as 120 days) or it will then become subject to the 10% IRA penalty.

Be knowledgeable about the options available for Native Americans. If you are Native American and are a first time home buyer, you can actually apply for what is known as the Section 184 Loan. With this loan, you will need about

1.5 % up-front guarantee fee and a down payment of only 2.25% for loans that rise above $50,000. If your loan falls below $50,000, the down payment required is only 1.24%. There is more to it however: a traditional loan will fix your interest rates based on what your credit score is. This is scrapped, with regard to the Section 184 Loan. The interest rate attached to your loan will be based only on the rate of the prevailing market. However, even as a Native American, you can only apply a Section 184 Loan for a residential property (maximum of 4 units) and for primary residences.

Here is something else: throw away all that talk about "loyalty to my current bank" out the window when it comes to buying your first home. What does it have to do with you arriving at the best deal possible? If your credit score has taken a hit for one reason or the other, despite being a loyal and good customer, do you think that your current financial institution will go out of their way and allow you the options of somebody with an excellent credit score? They will not. Do not be tied by loyalty to your local bank or current financial institution when you are seeking out a mortgage/pre-approval. Shop around as much as you can, regardless of whether you only qualify for one type of loan. You may be surprised to learn that fees often vary, and by significant rates as well, which has an impact on the total amount you end up paying. If your current bank caps your loan amount and refuses to consider lending you more, or has an above average loan interest rate, there is nothing wrong with seeking another financial suitor. Put yourself first, just like you are sure the bank is putting itself first.

Some pros will recommend that you line up a back-up lender. And it is not such a bad idea. Why is this? Well, qualifying for a loan does not always guarantee that your loan will get funded. There are several things that, if they shift, can alter your situation, such as lender risk-analysis, underwriting guidelines and the state of investor markets. There have been cases of borrower's signing all the necessary documents for their mortgage, only to be notified 24 hours before the mortgage closing that the lending has been frozen due to any number of reasons. In such a situation, lining up a 2nd lender's pre- approval gives you another option to run with, if the first one fails to work. However, it rarely is the case that a pre-approval gets overturned. Still, it does not hurt to know as much as possible.

#3: Make An Offer

Here, your buyer specialist will inform you on just how much money you should offer the seller for the house, as well as any other conditions you can ask for. If you are of the same mind, the buyer specialist will then approach

the seller, or the representative he or she is employing, and table the offer that the both of you agreed upon. The seller may then either accept your offer or respond with an offer of their own, referred to as a counter-offer. You may then accept this offer or opt to go back and forth until you either get to a deal or decide to let it go and focus on something else.

Before you submit your offer, however, take a close look at your budget and see where you stand. Costs often tend to accumulate; such costs as commuting costs, immediate repairs that must be made and compulsory appliances that you have to have fitted before moving in could cause you to spend far more money than you intend to.

Think ahead too: it is very easy, when dealing with homes, to get surprised by utility costs that you did not expect at all, especially if you are moving into a home that is larger than your current space. A good place to start is to request the home's energy bills from the past year or so, so that you get an idea of what the monthly bills look like.

Once you reach an agreement, you will then make what is known as a "good- faith deposit", which leads to the entire process transitioning into escrow. Escrow is basically a short time period (usually 30 days/1 month) where the house seller will take the house out of the market, with the expectation (this has to be expressed in writing) that you are buying the house, so long as you do not discover serious flaws that the seller may have hidden from you.

#4: *Close Or Move On To Greener Pastures*

If you are able to settle on a deal with your seller, via your buyer specialist preferably, and the home inspection (covered in this very part of the book) reveals no major flaws that put you off the deal, you are now ready to close the deal. Basically, closing involves signing lots of paperwork, and in a considerably short time period too, while keeping your fingers crossed that it does not all bottom-out at the last minute.

There are things that you will be required to handle in these final stages, and perhaps pay for. They may include:

- Having the prospective home appraised (mortgage companies are especially vigilant with this one, as their interest is on the line)

- Performing a title search, so that you make sure there is no other seller on the scene, peddling the house around

- Getting a private mortgage insurance program if you cannot help it that your down payment falls below 20%. Remember that in the long run, such an arrangement will cost you more than if you had gone the traditional way.

- Completing the mortgage paperwork

- You may also require to front loan-origination fees, surveys, title insurance, credit report fees and taxes.

The next phase of the home buying process is inspection.

INSPECTING THE HOME: WHAT CAN YOU EXPECT?

Regardless of how perfect your choice of home appears; regardless of this book's insistence on moving with speed when it comes to buying a house, it is extremely vital that you allow a concise and thorough home inspection process to be carried out. There have been home buyers who were excited to own their new homes only to discover major flaws that either significantly devalued the home, or were very costly to fix. Seeing as you are paying good money for the home, why not make sure you get your value for money? For a thorough home inspection process, make sure to hire a qualified professional home inspector.

How many days from acceptance/full closing should the home inspection be complete?

The timeframe here varies from state to state but generally, it should be about 10 business days. It is important that you schedule the home inspection within the timeframe required; otherwise, even though you discover flaws later on, it will be difficult to make a case of abandoning the purchase, since you failed to follow the rules. Do not be content with letting your home home inspector take care of all the details of the home inspection while you do other things; this is your home after all, and it makes all the sense in the world to be present when the process is being carried out. Most competent home inspectors understand how to carry out a home inspection but in case they are too swamped, they will hire a competent home inspector to ensure you get a proper home.

What is the purpose of the home inspection?

Certainly, it is vital that inspection of the home mechanicals front the inspection, and the home inspector's/buyer specialist's job here, first and foremost, is to ensure that they all work just fine. Buying a house with a broken furnace will mean that you spend money down the line on fixing it, or endure hell when winter rolls around. The mechanicals will include:

- Furnace
- AC
- Plumbing
- Roof
- Electricity and wiring

However, having an evaluation of the mechanical elements of the house is not all the home inspector should do. It is the inspector's job to look at every component of the house and determine how well each is holding up:

- Are the windows intact? If there are any broken windows, is the damage minimal or is large scale refitting necessary?
- Is the dishwasher in god condition? Does it look well maintained?
- What is the condition of the kitchen sink? Is there some blockage? Does the sink tap water run in sufficient volume?
- What is the state of the walls? Is the paint or wallpaper peeling away? And if this is the case, will the repairs involve too much work and financing?
- What is the state of the floors? Are they cracked or intact? Do they appear freshly done up? If there is carpeting available, what is its state? Are there stains on it that will be hard to eliminate?

All this gives you an idea on the kind of wholesome job the home inspector is expected to carry out. This is why a proper home inspection will rarely ever take a short time.

How long should your home inspector/buyer specialist take?

A proper inspector will take two to three hours inspecting the home, regardless of how well maintained it looks. The same goes for condos, flats and any other property type you may be looking for. You may expect your inspector to have a look at everything from the outside-in. He or she will thoroughly inspect the roof. The inspector will look at the attic and the basement. This will be your chance to familiarize yourself on what the home inspector looks for. Ask as many questions as possible and carry a notebook to write down some notes. This will also be your home too, so it will help that you glean as much as possible.

What kind of things ought to worry you, going by the inspection?

There are some things that, while unappealing to see, ought not to worry you too much. A blocked sink will be easily fixed by a plumber for little money. A lawn space that is a bit unkempt can be fixed easily if you are willing to roll your sleeves up and get to work with a blade and shovel. However, there will be other things that you observe that will worry you, and rightly so. Here are a few of them:

- **Major mechanical elements in a poor or underwhelming condition:**

These are the most vital components to look out for and they should draw the most concern from you. What is the state of the AC? Is it broken? If it is, will it take too much to fix? The air conditioning is dysfunctional- is the area hot enough to warrant worry over this? Does the roof leak? What is the overall situation of the plumbing? Work with your inspector so that all of them are looked at thoroughly.

- ***Wall state or wall decorations are in a poor condition:***

We are not talking about being dissatisfied with the white wallpaper present as you prefer yellow wallpaper, despite the wallpaper being in great condition. You can tweak this in due time. We are talking about peeling wall paint or wallpaper that is all torn up and requires immediate overhauling. Once you get to this stage of the deal, only to discover some of these things, understand that the seller will usually be unwilling to make the necessary changes. He or she may have no problems in replacing a dysfunctional furnace or AC but it will usually not be the case with wall decorations. If you feel you should get better, raise the issue up with the seller.

- ***Some minor conditions that could go either way:***

A broken window seal is not too big a deal, as is a leaky faucet. However, if there are too many broken window seals and broken faucets around, it may cost you more than you are ready to spend on repairs. Raise the issue up with the seller via your inspector/buyer specialist.

Next, we will be discussing the ins and outs of closing the deal having checked all the points we've already discussed.

CLOSING THE DEAL

The Concept Of "Earnest Money" Deposit

As a home buyer, you will be required to pay an earnest money deposit, once you have come across property that appeals to you, and that you intend to close. The earnest money deposit is something that confuses many first time home buyers. "After all," they ask, "Am I not already paying a down payment? Why do I have to pay an earnest money deposit on top of that?" The earnest money deposit, however, is not just another closing cost that is only there to help bleed your purse dry. Let us look at it, what it means and how you can protect it.

What Is An Earnest Money Deposit?

It is what we could call a "deposit in good faith". It is not to be confused with the down payment, though it is part of it. When you execute a purchase contract as a buyer, it will specify just how much money you will put up initially to secure that contract. This money amount will display good faith, and it will show that you are indeed serious about purchasing the home. This amount of money is the earnest money deposit. While we could call it part of the down payment, you will pay up this amount before you put down the down payment at closing. It is money that, besides showing good faith, secures the purchase contract.

How Much Money Is Enough For The Earnest Money Deposit?

There is no set requirement and usually, the seller will determine just how much it is, via his or her representative. However, absurdly low deposit amounts, such as $1.00 or $5.00 make it difficult for legal recognition and approval. And if anything, offering the seller's rep $1.00 as earnest money marks you out as even more of a joker than the guy who is unwilling to pay any at all.

A lot of the time, you will be required to pay 1% to 3% of the sales price. It will be very rare to be called upon to pay up more than 3%. You will only be called upon to pay up more than 3% if the seller's market is full of buyers fighting over a limited property pool. You can see why it would make sense for this to happen.

Protecting Your Earnest Money Deposit

Many first time home buyers have lost their earnest money deposit by not being smart about whom they are giving it to. A lot of the time when you give it to somebody untrustworthy, who then vanishes with it, it will be quite difficult to get it back even if you have the police helping you. And you will likely lose more in legal fees, if you catch up with the crook and take them to court.

Here is what you must do to keep your deposit safe:

- Never give your earnest money deposit directly to the seller.

- Make this deposit payable via a 3rd party that is reputable. You should use a well-known real estate brokerage, a legal firm, an escrow company or a title company. This way, the money is kept safe and is only distributed at closing.

The other thing we will discuss is negotiating the contract.

The Process Of Negotiating The Contract: What Do You Do?

You may be lucky and have the seller accept your first offer with no fuss at all. If this happens, you will not have to go through a negotiating process, which is just fine. However, it will be extremely rare for this to go down, especially if the seller brings along his own representative, who will be pushing for the best possible price. This is why you should know what the contract negotiation process looks like and what it entails. This section walks you through the primary items.

Item #1: Evaluating The Seller's Offer

When the seller, via his or her own rep, presents their offer, take your time to go through each bit with your buyer specialist. Go through every section with a fine toothcomb, making sure to seek clarification from your buyer specialist where necessary. Your buyer specialist will help you understand all the terms as well as openings in the contract that present opportunities for your own counter offer.

Pay great attention to these details:

- When is closing scheduled and just when can you take possession?
- Are there some deadlines that the seller, via their rep, considers important?

Item #2: Taking Care Of Contingencies

The most common one is the mortgage contingency. As a buyer, this book has stressed the importance of making an offer only after pre-qualification by your lender, as this helps you save everybody's time, including your own. You will also know exactly how much you can afford to offer to the seller.

Other contingencies to take care of may include attorney review, home inspections, prepaid costs and repairs- we have dedicated significant content in the book to explain them. It is important to consider that each will be bound by a time frame, which you must adhere to. The best way to take care of contingencies is to ensure you at least have about 5% of the total price amount free to use, not counting the down payment you are making.

Item #3: Coming Up With A Price That Favors All Parties

This is where your buyer specialist really gets to shine. As your representative and personal shopper, your buyer specialist is tasked with getting a fair price for you. However, even as he or she aims for the lowest price possible, it must not be so absurdly low that you risk annoying the seller and losing out on the purchase contract.

Settling on a price is a back and forth process. However, it requires both parties to respond to counter offers by specific dates. It does not mean that you wait until the specified date; it means that you cannot wait past that date to reply.

Here are some tips to help you come up with the best offer possible for both parties:

- Take a co-operative approach. This means an approach that includes both your buyer specialist and the seller's own representative. Seek to understand why the seller is pricing the house the way he/she is and consult with your buyer specialist on what price makes the most sense.

- Keep an open mind. The first way to succeed at this is to be open to paying a little more than you were prepared to do. The 2nd way is to be prepared to walk away; regardless of how appealing the property is, if the pricing is unfavorable.

- Be flexible. This means that you are willing to haggle and settle on a middle point, with regard to closing costs involved. Being too rigid on your price may see you lose out on great property in a great neighborhood.

Now that you know what you need to be aware of when negotiating for a deal, let's now get to the closing part; what exactly happens? That's what we will be discussing next.

What Exactly Happens At A Closing?

You have worked with your buyer specialist and have eventually found a home that suits your needs as well as your tastes. After some expected negotiations with the seller over the pricing, your offer has been accepted and barring any mishaps, the home should be yours in due time. You also have the requisite money: you went to the bank a while ago and have since had your pre- approval. All that remains between you and the home is the closing process. This section simplifies the home closing process to the point where it is easily understandable.

What Exactly Is Real Estate Closing?

Closing is sometimes referred to as settlement. It will be the final step of the real estate transaction. The closing process revolves around the proceeds of the sale being distributed to the home seller and the home's title being handed over to the buyer from the seller. This is where the fruit of your hard work will show- it is the point where you tie up all the loose threads together, settle all the necessary elements and be able to own your home.

Closing is usually handled by a 3rd party that is neutral such as a real estate attorney or title company. These 3rd parties are collectively referred to as closing agents, and their job, besides seeing to it that the deal goes through, is to ensure that both parties get the best deal possible. The closing agent, in all honesty, will be looking out for you way more than they are the seller. This is because money is straightforward enough- a transaction regarding money is as simple as they come. With property exchange however, there may be title issues that complicate the sale. It could be that the house is owned by yet another party, which could see you in court and your purchase invalidated. The closing agent ensures everything is in order before giving the green light.

What is it that goes on at closing?

The major events that are carried out at closing are inclusive of:

- The title of the home, as well as the house keys, getting transferred from the seller to the buyer
- The sale proceeds being distributed to the seller
- The buyer signing the mortgage note, if the home is already financed
- The buyer, or even the seller, settling such costs as real estate commissions, property taxes and title insurance among others

Simply put, the events listed above will be the most important ones, regarding closing, and the closing process will be built around them.

Let's take the discussion further by discussing the closing process in detail:

Comprehending Your Closing Process

Like we said earlier in the book, closing involves a lot of paperwork. This is inclusive of the deed, which will grant legal rights and will be signed by the home seller before being given to the buyer. The deed then has to be registered with the county or city so that the ownership rights of the new owner are sufficiently protected. Keys to your new house will also be handed to you, but you already knew that.

To wrap everything up, the home seller will receive a check for the proceeds of the transaction. The proceeds are referred to as net proceeds, seeing as such costs as closing costs and what the seller may owe on his or her original loan will be subtracted.

The HUD-1 Settlement Statement

The financial details of the transactions that will occur at the closing process will be summarized in the HUD-1 Settlement Statement, which is the document where all financial details regarding real estate closing should be included. This makes the transaction legally recognized by the government.

As a buyer, it is very important that you review this document. Well, the same goes for the seller, but this book can only make recommendations to its target audience; the home buyers. You are obligated to receive the document a minimum of 1 day before the closing process. It is obviously more ideal if you can access the document several days before closing, as this will give you more time to review it.

The HUD-1 will show, line by line, every expense as well as who will pay what amount. The reason you must review the HUD-1 is so that you know exactly what you are paying for.

As the home buyer, you can expect to pay your share of closing costs as well as escrow fees (we have talked about this in the book). It will be necessary to bring a cashier's check for the balance of the amount you owe for the closing costs, as the HUD-1 shows. The next chapter will focus on just how much money you require to have to close.

Go Through Every Closing Step Carefully

You will likely be very excited and will want to finalize transactions as swiftly as possible. However, it will be in your best interests to take your time, as any number of things could go wrong. Let us look at the HUD-1 statement for example: the document is several pages long as it has to address every transaction involved. There could very well be errors within and you could find yourself paying for more than you owe.

What should you bring at closing?

As a first time buyer, your buyer specialist and the lender to some extent should have provided you with ample coaching on what you ought to bring to the closing. In the majority of cases, you will need:

- The big check: You will need to bring a cashier's check, not a personal one, for the full amount dictated by the HUD-1. This will be inclusive of down payments as well as closing costs.

- Personal checkbook: You will fancy being in a position where you can cover last minute changes, if need be. It may also be necessary to cut your seller a check for some items that may not have been included in the settlement; such settlements as heating oil left in the tank and such kind.

- Your full attention: There will be a lot of paperwork to sign during closing, and it may all be very intimidating. Your buyer specialist will certainly be a big help here but this does not mean delegating everything to them: get involved in the paperwork- this is your house after all, is it not? If you require clarification, do not be afraid to ask for it.

How Much Cash Is Really Needed To Close On A Home?

To buy a home, you will need the requisite cash for the down payment, and then some more. This chapter looks at just how much money you will need on hand so as to have a smooth closing process and fully purchase your new home.

As a first time home buyer, you may feel deflated at discovering that you need significantly more cash than just the down payment you make. It is difficult enough having to save for a 20% down payment on the home, only to discover that you need more so as to finalize the transaction. However, this is the way it is with every home buyer, and it has been that way since home buying became a thing.

Let us take a look at just how much cash it will take to buy your home. Where possible, we will suggest ways that may reduce or even nullify the additional costs.

#1: The actual down payment

This one is the most obvious one; even the first time home buyer should have it as an obvious expenditure. As we have covered in this book, it will be expressed as a percentage of the total buying price of the house. For instance if your house purchase price is $100,000 and you are to make a down payment of 20%, you will have to fork out $20,000.

#2: The Closing costs

The down payment is easy enough to understand, as it is very straightforward. When it comes to the closing costs, however, things start to become a little complicated. This is seeing as the cash outlay to make the buy often gets a lot higher than just the down payment.

Here is a stat that may terrify you; closing costs can run up to 3% of your entire loan amount.

This means that on, say, a $200,000 mortgage, you may be required to come up with an extra $6,000, in addition to the down payment you are expected to make.

Closing costs tend to vary from one state to the next. This may be due to differences in property transfer tax and mortgage "stamps" (these are government taxes that are collected based on a certain % of the total mortgage loan amount). Another reason they vary is that there are different rates that are charged for attorneys, title insurance and even appraisals.

Closing costs may also vary from one lender to another; even from one loan to the next. How is this? Well, different lenders will charge different application fees. To add to this, your lender may charge mortgage points (covered in part 1 of this book). Mortgage points are named as such seeing as a point represents a percentage point of your mortgage amount. 1 point equals 1% of the total loan amount.

With regard to closing costs, you have 2 alternatives that will either drastically cut down on your closing costs or nullify them altogether:

1. Negotiate, via your buyer specialist, so that the seller carries the closing costs himself. This, however, is only legal in areas where this is practiced commonly.

2. Negotiate a premium pricing with your bank or lender. The trade-off is simple here: the lender will foot your closing costs and in return, you will pay a higher rate of interest on your mortgage.

Both alternatives are great- your choice will depend on your circumstances.

#3: Pre-paid expenses

Prepaid charges will probably prove to be your most confusing charges. However, no matter how much this is the case, you must approach them as completely necessary charges.

With the majority of mortgages, your lender will place the real estate taxes as well as your insurance in escrow. The meaning of this is that these charges will be added up to your monthly loan payments. The lender pays them off when they are due.

So that this is possible, your lender will need to collect certain money amounts upfront, so as to ensure that funds are available to make the payments, when they are due. Escrow accounts will be set up to take care of the charges that the next due date brings, while a portion of the monthly payments you make supplements the escrow account, for the next due date after that.

Depending on the place you live in and the tax frequency, with regard to real estate tax collecting, your lender may be compelled to put up to 12 months of real estate tax in escrow. If the taxes charged on the house are $250 a month, this translates to a pre-paid expense of $1,500.

#4: Utility adjustments

These may be inclusive of a large number of charges. The good news, however, is that they rarely ever exceed a few hundred dollars. Basically, utility adjustment costs will represent the utility costs that are paid by your seller in advance.

Let us go back to an example we used the previous chapter: if your seller had re-filled the heating oil tank before the closing process, you are required to reimburse him or her for this unused oil, unless they decide to waive that cost. Similar charges may be incurred if the seller has also prepaid other utilities such as sewer removal or trash removal.

#5: Lender-requisite "cash reserves"

This particular one takes a lot of home buyers by surprise. Actually, it is not a closing expense, seeing as you do not lose it to anyone. But your lender will require that you at least have a certain amount of money in savings after all the closing costs have been taken care of. Otherwise, the lender will just pull out of lending your money, since it makes no financial sense to lend to someone who has too little money in his account. Lenders uphold this requirement, in their own words, to "avoid the buyer closing broke."

The most typical requirement of cash reserve is 2 months. This means that you at least have sufficient money in your account to cover the first 2 months of your mortgage payments. Thus, if the principal, taxes, interest and insurance total to $2,000, your reserve requirement is $3,000.

Let's take the discussion further.

Everything You Need To Know About the Various Closing Costs as a New Home Buyer

Basically, what this will do is outline the various closing costs you may come across, especially in the HUD-1, and explain to you what they mean. At least this way, you will have a good idea what a particular closing cost is, and not be surprised when you find it among other more obvious closing costs.

#1: Flood Hazard Certificate

This one means exactly what its naming suggests. Your seller is expected to provide certification that shows whether the home she is selling is in the flood plain or not. This brings us to the following: if the house you are purchasing is indeed in the flood plain, you are required by law to buy flood insurance. And no, you cannot do it at a later date- you have to pay up at closing.

#2: Application fee

You will pay this one to your lender before closing. This fee pays for the house to be "appraised professionally". In addition, the flat $50.00 credit report fee that is required from your lender will be paid from this particular fee.

#3: Wire transfer fee

This will only be applicable on some loans. If the situation is such that you cannot arrive at the seller's with your cashier's check to close, and your lender has to wire the amount, this fee will be applied and you will be the one footing it. It will be paid at closing.

#4: Survey fee

Remember when we said that it is extremely important to have the property surveyed so that you do not have to deal with boundary disputes with neighbors down the line? Well, a proper survey will have to involve a surveyor, whom you can access via your buyer specialist. He or she will record exactly where your house sits on the lot and where the boundaries are placed. You will get a copy of the survey at closing, and you will be required to pay the survey fee shortly after. Also, understand that this is not a "pin survey", which takes a lot more time and is a lot more expensive.

#5: Courier fee

There are times when your lender or bank is required to courier certain documents, relative to the house you are buying. A lot of the time, this is necessary to obtain some final signatures to properly wrap the entire deal up. If this is necessary, your lender will bill you for courier costs.

#6: Lender processing fee

Well, this one varies somewhat, and your lender may opt to spread it over into some other charge. However, if it is in your HUD-1, it points to the charge that your lender puts in place for putting the transaction together. Simply put, your lender is billing you for making it possible for you to purchase your house. You could call it one extra way for your lender to make a profit. Sometimes however, this fee is channeled toward the processor for putting together and packaging all your necessary documents, so that everything attains a professional look and fee.

#7: Home inspection fee

We have already looked at home inspection, so you should be expecting this one. Part of the reason why this book recommends you to be present for the home inspection is that you are expected to pay this particular fee at the time of the inspection. You do not pay the home inspection fee at closing- you pay it way before closing, immediately the inspection is completed.

#8: Broker processing fee/governmental compliance fee

This is the fee that is paid to the broker. This fee is applied to the "preparation of documents relative to the closing, their processing and ultimately their storage." This fee will be paid at closing.

#9: Title company closing fee

We mentioned in the previous chapter that it is vital to involve a title company or an attorney with professional experience and credentials in the field, as it ensures that you get a deal that is not flawed by such title issues as having more than one owner having the property in his or her ownership. You will be expected to pay a fee to the Title Company or attorney, for processing your closing documents in a professional capacity. You will pay the fee at closing.

#10: Title insurance binder

This insures that you are buying property from your seller that has no liens, a clear title and basically, no ownership complications that will jeopardize your very own ownership in the future.

#11: Title insurance lender's policy

This one applies to your lender, even though the fee is paid to the title company and not to lender/bank. This insures your bank or lender that they are indeed lending on a property with no legal complications.

#12: EPA endorsement

This one insures that you are not buying property that is hazardous or harmful to you and your family's health in any way. It is not just another random fee however- there have to be checks made to see that there are no toxic materials on the property, or buried in it.

#13: ARM or balloon endorsement

If you have an ARM/balloon loan, then your lender will require you to have additional documents relative to these unique loans. The documents will basically explain what ARM and balloon payments mean in your capacity. You will need to furnish the lender with a fee for processing and availing these documents.

The other thing we are going to cover is how to win bidding wars in situations where a property is in high demand.

THE SECRETS TO COMING OUT ON TOP IN A BIDDING WAR

This is the home buying situation that every home buyer fears: You have found property that pretty much checks all your boxes. Barring perhaps one or two minor elements, the property pretty much fits your ideal dream home. In your mind, you can picture just how you will make it look- you know exactly what carpeting you want in place and you know exactly what kind of wallpaper you will install. The only thing that is left is to make an offer via your buyer specialist, have it accepted and put a close to the home's financing.

However, to your dismay, you discover that somebody else fancies the home just as much as you do. Worse still, you find out that they have offered more money to the seller. Effectively, a real estate bidding war has begun, and you are only a first time buyer with little experience in real estate. What do you do? How do you make sure you end up with the house, even though you cannot offer as much as the other guy is doing for it?

For starters, here is something you need to know:

The highest offer is not always the one that is accepted!

This is something that is not covered enough times- it is not always the highest offer that gets accepted. The offer that always gets accepted is the most APPEALING one. And yes, you can make your offer the most appealing one without it being the highest. Here are some tricks that you can implement to ensure that your offer is superior to the other bidder's, even if it is lower:

The strategies of winning a bidding war:

#1: Kill the conditions

The first step to take is to scour through the closing paperwork and eliminate as many conditions (such as "contingent upon results of a home inspection" or other conditions to that effect) from your offer. The seller will take notice of this, especially if you alert him or her to it and will seriously consider having you buy the property. (To have a deeper understanding on such conditions as "contingent upon results of a home inspection", check out the next chapter on financing clauses in the closing paperwork).

#2: Take care of the formalities

We are talking about humane formalities, not those associated with deal-making and closing. Take time to meet the homeowner and say hello. Ask about their 3 year old son or their pet: basically, find something of interest to the owner and seek to bond over it. Have you ever heard of the saying that people will prefer to do business with only those they like? Have the homeowner like you, and consider you a strong fit for the neighborhood. If it is impossible to meet the homeowner, you can just write a letter to the seller to introduce yourself then mail the letter along with your offer.

#3: Give the seller sufficient time

This is yet another simple yet very effective strategy. The date of "buyer possession" is usually a critical component of the deal. The seller may need to take care of a few home-related things before he/she can move out. He/she may need to spend a few days moving into his/her new home, or may be attached by sentiment to his/her old home. Add 3 or so more days to the moving-out date without asking for any compensation.

#4: Increase your earnest money

We have already covered earnest money earlier in the book. It will be tough forking out thousands of dollars, on top of your down payment and other closing fees but it may be exactly what you need to ensure the house is yours. If a seller has two competitive offers, he or she may feel significantly more secure going with the offer that has a larger earnest money deposit, as it appears that buyer is more serious about purchasing.

#5: Get pre-approved

Selling a house is rarely ever a small deal- sellers are quite often nervous that financing will fall through, which is why a lot of them tend to accept cash offers for less than offers that require financing. Even though you know your credit score is excellent, it may be very difficult to compete with someone buying in cash. However, you will improve the odds of you winning the bid by having a mortgage pre-approval in your hand. It will display to the seller that a bank has already viewed you as suitable for lending to, and is willing to give you the required amount of money.

If, for one reason or another, you do not have the necessary paperwork in order to get your pre-approval, you should at the very least show up for bidding with your letter of mortgage prequalification attached with your letter. Any bank will be able to process such a letter for you in less than 10 minutes.

Next, we will talk about how to handle counter offers.

Handling Counter Offers

It is important to understand that even the best offers often get countered by the seller. A counter offer simply means that while the seller would love to accept your offer, there are some changes that he or she would like to see in it.

For instance, you may offer to buy the home at $300,000 with a 20% down payment but you state that the seller must foot the bill for the termite damage repairs, prior to the escrow's close. The seller may counter by saying that he will accept your $300,000 with a down payment of 20%, but you will have to handle the termite repair yourself.

You may either choose to accept the counter-offer or back out of the deal and look for another home to buy. Understand that in real estate, counter-offers are rarely looked at as revisions of the original offer: they are considered new contracts in themselves. Thus, you should make sure that you read the contract very carefully.

It is often easy to get swept up in a bidding war- after all, you love the house and it feels real good to win. However, understand that it is just a house, when all is said and done. Always keep tabs on just how much you can afford or are comfortable spending on the house. If you are uncomfortable with the financial demands in place, it is wise to back out. By and by, you will find a place that suits you better, going by both your taste and your wallet.

If you've won the bidding war, the other thing you should understand is the various financing clauses involved in the home purchase process.

FINANCING CLAUSES: A LOOK AT THE VARIOUS FINANCING CLAUSES AS YOU WILL FIND THEM IN THE CLOSING PAPERWORK

For starters, let us look at the term "clause" so that you can understand the contents of this chapter better. The term clause points to specifics in a deal; specifics of either money or a time frame of operation. With a financing clause, it points to specifics in financing, which is to mean a specific payable amount. However, as is expected, the timeframe is also a major factor in these clauses and penalties are often attached if violation of the timeframe stipulated is present. Think of a "release clause" in sports: a player will be let go if another professional club is willing to pay the exact price as dictated by the release clause. This price is supreme: if the buying party meets it and the player is keen on a move, there is little the selling party can do.

Certainly, financing clauses in sports rarely ever work the same way as in real estate, but you get the point- if you, for example, sign with the seller on a certain cash clause, the seller cannot then bump up his price in the future, as he or she is legally bound by the cash clause. Neither can you decide to pay less than the amount dictated by the cash clause, as you are legally bound to it as well.

Let us look at some of the various financing clauses, as they will be depicted in the closing paperwork. This will help you be prepared, once you advance all the way to the closing stage:

#1: Cash clause

By and large, this is how it will appear:

"The purchase price will be set at $_____. The buyer is to provide verification of the necessary funds to buy the property, suitable to the seller, within_____calendar days. Failure to follow both stipulations in money amount and time will result in the pre-agreed deal getting declared null and void.

#2: Conventional loan clause

The conventional loan clause will read like this:

"This contract is contingent upon the buyer obtaining a loan commitment, in an amount that does not exceed (insert a definite % such as 70%) of the buying price within _____calendar days. After acceptance, hereof application will be made within__days of the offer's acceptance.

#3: FHA loan clause

This one will read like this:

"This contract is contingent upon the home buyer obtaining a loan commitment that is insured by the FHA, with the inclusion of MIP, within __calendar days after the offer has been accepted."

#4: VA loan clause

It will read like this:

"This contract is contingent upon the home buyer obtaining a loan commitment guaranteed by the VA, within calendar days after acceptance.

The application is to be made within _____ calendar days after acceptance of the offer. The buyer will avail the *funding fee of the VA."*

#5: Loan assumption clause

This clause will read like this:

"The buyer will assume the existing mortgage of the seller, with an approximated balance of $_____ at an interest of_____ %, with years remaining, and monthly payments totaling $_____ , which is inclusive of the principal, interest, tax, insurance for hazards as well as mortgage insurance. The buyer will avail the loan assumption fee, along with the necessary closing costs. The seller/buyer is expected to make the monthly payment as is scheduled, following the date of closing. The buyer will buy the seller's escrow account, which will be current at the time of closing. The necessary taxes will be probated accordingly."

Optional: *"The seller will choose to assign the escrow account to the buyer, rather than have him or her purchase it, so as to help the buyer have a lighter financial load, considering there will be tax probation."*

#6: Mortgage by seller financing clause

This clause will read like this:

"The home buyer's obligation to buy is contingent upon the home seller providing necessary financing to the buyer, evidenced by a note and secured by a 1st mortgage. This note shall be in the amount of $_____based on a term of_____years, at an interest rate of_____ _%. The entire unpaid interest, which is inclusive of both the principal and the interest, will be due and payable at the end of_____ years. The buyer may prepay

the entire amount at any time without any penalty in the offing.

This note shall contain a ____ day default period as well as a late charge of ____% if the payment is __ days late. Also in the event of lateness, the buyer/seller will foot the costs of preparation of all loan documents as well as the closing costs."

#7: Mortgage by seller (2nd mortgage) clause

"The buyer's obligations to buy are contingent upon the seller providing necessary financing to the buyer as evidenced by a note secured by a 2nd mortgage on the premises of the subject. This note will be in the amount of

$_____, based on a term of_____ years and at an interest rate of _____%. The entire unpaid balance, which is inclusive of the principal as well as interest, shall be payable at the end of_____ years. The buyer may prepay the entire amount at any time without risk of penalty. This note shall contain a _____ day default period as well as a late charge of _____% if the payment is_____days late. Also in the event of lateness, the buyer/seller will foot the costs of preparation of all loan documents as well as the closing costs."

#8: Land Contract Clause

"The purchase is contingent upon the seller granting a land contract in the amount of $_____, with a down payment of $_____, based on a term of____years and at an interest rate of_____ years. The buyer may prepay the entire amount at any time without risk of penalty. This note shall contain a _____ day default period as well as a late charge of _____% if the payment is____days late. Also in the event of lateness, the buyer/seller will foot the costs of preparation of all loan documents as well as the closing costs."

Finally, we will talk about what you need to do as a new homeowner.

ACTION AS A NEW HOME OWNER

You have now graduated from a new home buyer to a new home owner... now

what?

You have signed the papers, made payments to the movers and finally moved in. By and by, the new place is starting to feel like home. It is all over, right? You can now sit back and uncross your legs on a job finally completed, no? Actually, you cannot quite do this. What you have done, by ending your time as a home buyer, is become a home owner, complete with all the responsibilities that come with it. Homeownership costs, for starters, always tend to extend beyond the down payment and the monthly payments toward settling your mortgage. In this chapter, we will examine tips that will help ease you into homeownership and provide more fun and security to it.

#1: Keep saving

Homeownership comes with some unexpected expenses that can be quite considerable in amount. You could find out that your roof needs more than just repair at points; that it needs to be torn down wholly and replaced. You could find out that the water heater is ruined and you have to install a new one soon, especially with winter coming up. Start some emergency fund for the home so that in the near future when costs start creeping up, you will be ready for them.

#2: Perform constant house maintenance

You are putting up a lot of money to buy your house in the first place. This means that it is one of your biggest assets, if not the biggest. It only makes sense, thus, to take excellent care of it. Regular checks and maintenance activity will vastly decrease repair costs, since you will fix any problems while they are still small and more manageable. There are also fewer ways to help you get familiar with your house better than performing maintenance checks. And the best part about it is that most of the checks and repairs are things that you can do yourself.

#3: The house market may mean nothing…or everything; it all depends on you

The point of this one is this; you need to ignore the housing market, something that too many first time home buyers and owners fail to do. It really matters not what your house is worth at a particular moment, until that moment that you decide to sell it off. You do not need to keep timing the market, or something else like that; being able to choose just when you sell your home, as opposed to being forced to sell due to "thinking the market is right" or due to financial strain, or something else like that, may be the biggest determinant whether you will get a solid profit from the investment and better yet, leave having utilized it to its maximum potential.

#4: If it was in your plans to use your home to fund your retirement, put a stop to that way of thinking

Even if you now own a home, which is quite an asset for anyone to have, and which will mostly only appreciate in value, it is important that you keep saving to the max for your retirement fund every year that passes. It is true that there are people who have made a killing from maneuvering their way through the housing bubble but it does not mean that you stand to make a killing from selling, just like they perhaps did. If you are looking at your home as a source of retirement wealth, there are a few things to consider.

For starters, the money that you are using to make monthly payments toward your mortgage could very well be used to fund living and medical expenses in your retirement. Think about this last point, especially.

CONCLUSION

We have come to the end of the book. Thank you for reading and congratulations for reading until the end.

This book is as comprehensive as they come. You are now armed with just about everything you need to go confidently about shopping for and buying a new house. Always remember that the time factor is almost always as important as the money factor when it comes to home buying. Take your time for sure, but do not take too much time. You should also consider that buying and owning a home will cost you a lot more than just your down payment: there are several closing costs to cover, not to mention you will have to spend on the house as a homeowner. Nevertheless, owning your first home is something to be immensely proud of. And by getting to the end of this book, it is clear that you are serious about home buying. All that remains now is to go out there, apply the nuggets of wisdom in this book and buy your ideal first home.

If you found the book valuable, can you recommend it to others? One way to do that is to post a review on Amazon.

Thank you and good luck!

www.ingramcontent.com/pod-product-compliance
Lightning Source LLC
Chambersburg PA
CBHW020453220526
45464CB00002B/974